It's Hard Being Queen

The Dusty Springfield Poems

It's Hard Being Queen

The Dusty Springfield Poems

Jeanette Lynes

Library and Archives Canada Cataloguing in Publication

Lynes, Jeanette

It's hard being queen : the Dusty Springfield poems / Jeanette Lynes.

ISBN 978-1-55111-926-7

1. Springfield, Dusty--Poetry. I. Title.

PS8573.Y6I87 2008 C811'.54 C2008-903543-7

Freehand Books
412 – 815 1st Street SW
Calgary, Alberta
Canada T2P 1N3
www.freehand-books.com

Book orders
Broadview Press Inc.
280 Perry Street, Unit 5
Peterborough, Ontario
Canada K9J 7H5
phone: 705-743-8990
fax: 705-743-8353
customerservice@broadviewpress.com
www.broadviewpress.com

Printed in Canada

Freehand Books, an imprint of Broadview Press Inc., acknowledges the financial support for its publishing program from the Government of Canada through the Book Publishing Industry Development Program (BPIDP).

For the Writers of Saskatchewan —

You helped me hear the music again

Contents

I

Dust, Musings

(at an unspecified moment)

Who can explain the accidents of birth?
She could have been a speckled trout,
a peacock, diamond, boy. Her talents
went straight to her throat, her ears
(dimming her eyes, her fans in later
years a screamy blur of love). If, falling
from her pram, she'd died, there'd *be*
no fans. Who can know the figments
of life, its angers? Her father's fingers
leafing through tax blanks, should have
shaken some concert hall's ivory keys.
Her mother numbed by a drug called
Technicolor, lost in the movie house.
The adolescent monster in the mirror,
her – a girl no good at swimming,
Jane Austen, or anything.
Who can predict when the glass
will finally speak – *Open your mouth –*
reach deep into your throat, it's all
there: fish, bird, gem, boy, song.

Vision

She peers into mirrors.
Everyone thinks her vain, they're so amiss.
It's her eyes, she can barely see
a blessed thing. She squints harder
into the silver haze. Something's
wrong about the nose, the chin
wavers – ready – set – goes fleshy
at the least provocation. A wobble
of a face – and reputed to be hers.
Unblessed things are all she can see.
No choice but wait until the face
that shimmies back at her
belongs to Peggy Lee!

The Gospel Truth

The south is the place we use to prove that we are more real than we feel.

—Warren Zanes

Singers, her *real* family
lives across the ocean, now.
Severed at birth by some cosmic
muddle she's been
pale ever since. There's no day
she doesn't hear their call,
more cry than call
vaulting from the brittle
pages of cold testaments
from the fierce sheen of rowed corn
from fields larger than London
from mules set in relief against sunrises
merciless in their reds.
From bare tarnished soles. They sound
like only one's family can. God is stuck
in their throats. They pluck
their notes from gut fretted
across the hollow bellies of old barrels.
Someday she'll find them. Their songs
send her rushing to the atlas.
She knows better, of course. *Under* the map
is where they dwell. This doesn't daunt her
in the least. She lives to gaze
straight into their very mouths.

Only then will anything be real.

A Sonic Map of Childhood

Sirens swamp her crib. Air raids.
No one believes she remembers this
far back. Then the nightly spin of sound
from her father's room, Jelly Roll Morton.

Another room: *The Goon Show* blarking away.
Her brother mangling his guitar upstairs.
Jelly can't drown her parents' row,
her mother's Irish sobs. In their suburb

dark people from warm countries. Their deep music
enters her. She walks home past their flats so more
enters her. This means scolding for taking the long
way home. She doesn't care. Lots of reasons

for getting home late, this is only one of them.
No one ever believes her. Even when she grasps
the hot water pipes until her hands redden
and tells the people in their different rooms,

her scarlet palms raised, *look* – even *then* they don't
believe her. At least not enough to stop shouting,
bashing at innocent guitars, shattering crockery.
They've no inkling how far into the past her ears
extend. She can hear clear back to *cave families.*

She Takes a Hard Look at Herself

Mary O'Brien: ten, a bloody cow,
a tank of lard. National Health
spectacles squat enormous, round
on her bad nose. Her mother fired
another pie into the wall, little
to love in that house. Mary got mud
on her school uniform – her
brother likened her to a rolling
pig in dust. Her only real
accomplishment: she created the first
light show at her school.
The nuns, in their secret hearts,
liked it. That told her a great deal.
It told her Mary O'Brien
must die. She can take with her
only two things:
voice, dust.

Convent School

She keeps her head low, having lost
points for being hatless at Lourdes.
Even grottoes have laws. The others
are cross – she loses more points
she'll bring the whole house down.

Sister looked stern after asking
if she'd a calling – "Oh, yes,
blues singer." Sister said not
a fit vocation.

She creeps along the corridor,
reaches a door, Sister Fidelia's, closed.
Tobacco slithers under the door-slit,
right to her. She presses her magic ear
to the wood: Bessie Smith on the gramophone.
What Sister's doing in there would cost her

big points. God keeps score.
She'd plunge to zero to see
Fidelia's face right now, smitten
in Bessie's blue land. Closed doors
say more. This is what
she now knows: there's a face
behind every face, a road
at the end of the rules.

The Record Shop

1951. She strides forth, clears her throat:
"I'd like to make a record, please."
The shopkeeper bends over the counter
to better see her. He laughs. "Are you
legal?" "Of course not," she says,
"but I've got the quid so let me
make my record, maybe then they'll
believe me." "Who?" "My family."
Whoever she is, she saddens him –
one more war baby with bad nerves,
hundreds unhinged by that mess. Well
if it makes her feel better, why not?
Her song heaves from her throat –
When the Midnight Choo Choo Leaves
for Alabam. Just as he thought –
no child should sound so old so *dark* –
so *knowing* in a circus kind of way.
He wraps the grooves engrained
with her song. His hands shake.
For years the midnight choo choo
haunts his ears.

A Brief History of Vinyl

(later)

A record is a palimpsest, an incest
of sound. A drill-bit riding a carousel
at midnight. The world's most whopping
layer cake. Not even the piggiest
piglets among you can ever eat your way
to the bottom. The backtracks
have backtracks. Sound behind sound
behind sound. Rave all you want
about your good ears, they'll never
reach her record's acoustic back country
and what a blessing – Buddy Rich
is calling her a bitch, there, a limey
broad. That human thud you can't hear
is old Ida Metzger sailing onto Dusty's
roadster's hood. Then there's wretched
blubbering Mary O'Brien won't that
bloody cow stop and a myriad of other
frequencies you're not picking up –
the clanking of eyelashes finale
of teacups hitting the wall Martha Reeves
howling as sardines fly into her
exquisite cocoa collarbones.
You can't hear any of this.

High School Reunion

The vamp parted the waters
          when she walked in. Even the balloons
floated at attention. Her enormous
black-rimmed eyes scanned the room, all of London
          could be stashed in that hair.
Such mod
          saucy skirts, we could nearly see
her knees. She took one step after another
like her high-heeled feet followed a string
          along the floor to the punch bowl.

At last Sister Agnes extended her
          hand: "Hello, Mary." The vamp's
teeth blinded us. Could this be the drop-out,
our own plump Mary who pitched hockey
          loved pranks and picked tunes on guitar?
We thought she'd make

librarian at most. She'd been anointed
          like the rest of us, prayed at Lourdes
as we did, now this. We could only gawk
as she gabbled and sipped with the habitual
          nuns. When Sister Agnes said
"Give us a song, Mary" and she lowered
          her glass raised her voice in some

dark American torrent, it all came back to us:
          the rhythm method had always
meant something else to Mary O'Brien.

The Springfields

You can never be authentic if you're British. It's mimicry…
—Dusty Springfield

She's through singing at Butlin's Holiday Camp, done
with conga drums and hay. She won't wear fruit
in her hair, recline on one more bale.
She's no librarian in rockasilly skirts.
Bye to hill songs

sung in Latin twangs, bye to being so sodding
cheerful all the time. She's blowing that pop-stand,
that whole sonic suburb. She'd rather go mod
than mad. They don't know who she is.
She does and it's
a lot sadder
than they think.

She lightens her hair.

Darkens her voice.

Dirties the sound.

The Studio: Marble Arch

(London)

Session musicians. Play the notes, pocket their quid.
Never heard of Motown. They call her a beehived bird.

Her ears are ace. Onion juice cuts her throat open.
The sound? She wants it dark. Urgent. Chambered

and released. A breath breathing a breath breathing a breath.
Even if it means singing in the stairwell. The loo.

She's bored with dead Roman air, big-band daddies.
She ditches them for squalid stairs, a microphone

roped from the rafters. The echo she longs for – full
throttle at last – "You Don't Have to Say You Love Me."

A janitor with his bucket stumbles into her song. Even
when the singer waves, winks, he's terrified. No woman
sings like that. He must consult his chemist on dosage.

Some Facts About America

President: Burt Bacharach

Capital: Motown

Language: Twanglish

National Anthem: "Heat Wave"

Official drink: soda

Other Facts:

The flag is sewn from sequins.

A lady statue welcomes you,
you can see her wave from quite far away
even with weak eyes.

The lions are friendly there.

One hazard: walking with Billy-Ray.

They drive on the odd side. Right
through the wall of sound.

The middle class could install
a pool if they wanted to.

There are cities where people sing all day.
Sing their hearts out. Memphis being one.

There is a holy wood.

The Exciters

Her skirt skims her knees. Like all good skirts
it's moving up. She wears her swagger coat,
scoop-neck shell. New York is hell on heels
but she wouldn't be caught dead heel-less.
Best of all, they think she's one of them until
she opens her mouth for directions: Colony
Records. The store can't contain its own song,
"Tell Him." Girl voices rocket their relentless
driving riffs right onto the street. She loves
them so much her stockings tear, she doesn't care.
Nothing sounds like this where she's from.
A wall of wasted time wallops her heart.
Here's a country she could love. It's not ballads
she's needed, it's balls. She's sleepless
for days, that's the fever she's in, frantic
to follow her hem high as it can travel.

American Airwaves, 1964

Who's the new voice? Boxers lower their gloves. Typists stop typing.
Thunderbird roadsters burn rubber, eighteen-wheelers that didn't
down-shift in a hundred miles down-shift. Teacups in nursing homes
judder in arthritic fingers. Hands of wives beating cake batter
in Port Arthur, Texas, Port Arthur, Ontario, or any other Port Arthur
go stock still. Lesley Gore turns green. Even Barry Goldwater forgets,
for a moment, about being president.

It's crazy but it's true
I only want to be with you

Martha Reeves, buying skirts for the Vandellas, wonders why
she never heard this girl before. Martha doesn't miss much.
The girl can sing.

In his Los Angeles dressing room, Lloyd Thaxton gels his hair, countdown
to show time. He hums along, *wowzer* – the boy can carry a tune.
He scribbles a note: "This new Dusty – get him!"

Who can know the singer of the song? They hear husk, they think boy.
They hear bells, they think toy. They hear both.
Who can tell the colour of a voice?
They hear blue, they think black. They hear black, they think blue.
Or the new wonder-girls with their beehives, their dark, luminous eyes.

There's not a girl north of Galveston, south of Moose Factory,
east of Long Beach or west of Staten Island who doesn't wish
to be Dusty. Maybe not a boy, either. They tune their compasses,
attune to the wind's silken grit better than once they did.

Concert in South Africa, 1964

Her eyes are sunk in ponds of tar.
Kohl and mascara are for happy
mods, not bad girls
sent home by Ministers of Interiors
for singing to all
colours at once. Police in wings,
what's wrong, don't they like her songs?
They call her an alien, can't she be
like Vera Lynn and do what
she's told?

No. She has to be a rebel. Reigning Queen
of that island of long-hairs and freaks.
A martyr giving her pay to the poor
dark orphans oh boo hoo.
A ploy to be part of what coloureds
are stirring up in America,
sell more records.

Hate mail rains hard and white
down on her head. She won't be dry
for days. Kohl and mascara were never
invented for this.

It should be twenty years later
but it isn't. What she got for singing
to all colours: a boot up the ramp of a jet
and even when its passengers
press their hands together, clap
until it seems applause alone
will lift them above the bruised
tarmac, she weeps.

A Brief History of Mascara

The dark dream everyone dreamed first.
The living dust everyone believes
they invented. The Egyptians
wouldn't be caught dead
without it. *Mascara*, Spanish for mask
so naturally Spaniards claim
the wand. Citizens of Mascara, Algeria
say: hell we *live* here, it's *ours.*
Raccoons of the world, unite, take back
the 'hood! Back at the ranch
horses wear it – it's a cinch –
simply graze, lower your face into some
Santa Cruz tarweed then snog the earth,
an amicable collision of mammal and soil
known, in those parts, as The Mascara Effect.

Cut to Paris, 1840-something, Eugene Rimmel
ecstatic in a skirt, mixing his midnight cake.
Or later, Williams the chemist, pretending to be
his sister Mabel, dabbing his lashes
with Vaseline then coal dust. Must men insist
on inventing *everything*? Ziggy Stardust.
Marilyn Manson. Heavens Keith Richards.

The truth is, mascara has *royal* roots.
It wasn't born in coal at all, it belongs
to the queens. To Danny La Rue
being Dusty Springfield better than Dusty
could be herself. To Dusty being Danny
being Dusty on into perpetuity (this dance
is how the wand came to have its spiral –
they'll tell you it's for volume, length, *bosh*).

That's also why raccoons, when they snuffle
and root, go for anything that thickens,
that flutters, that shines.

You Know You've Made It When

She's all things to all
people, sure sign
the throne belongs
to her. She calls
the throne her own.

About time. All those
hillbilly skirts, how
bloody cheerful she's
had to be, now they
call her difficult.

Slotted between talking
dummy and Hungarian
acrobats by that dolt
Sullivan, who did they
remember? Dusty.

All the rest? Just more
bodies in flight, a hand
pushing a mouth. When
they demand boyfriends
she invents them, dresses

them in giggles. Boys
dream slide shows of who
maybe mussed her hair
on that album cover (they
did). Girls steal Dad's denim
shirt, strive to perfect
their own musses.

You've made it when America
swallows that's how
you look waking up.

The First Man on the Moon Hears Her on the Hi-Fi

Less and less holds him
there on earth. He hasn't yet landed his massive
boots on lunar
dust, but he will. He will. All the arresting wire
in the world can't
                    keep him down.

His wife understands
and doesn't.
                    All those accidents
he keeps having, she has to wonder
what he's wishing for.

There was that Joshua tree he fell
into from the sky. Doodads
continue to snap from
                    his flying machines.
Now he won't remove that silver suit,
even at night. He sleeps in the yard or
stares at the stars. The man she married
is a strand of oversized tinsel
out there.
                    No tail-hook

can hold him. She asks what it would take
to make him forget the moon. "A sweet
miracle of completely new
                    magnitude," he says.

She switches on the hi-fi – "Listen –
listen to Dusty." He shoots
his wife the first tender look in ages,
                                        a look of love. "That voice
would almost keep me here," he says.
"*Almost.*"

The Studio: Memphis

Dusty has entered the building, hairdresser
in tow. The musicians cackle – *yeah, in that*
rat 'n' roach crib they're in, a lady's hair
better be right. They throw their hands around,
cram the room with ghosts – this *very spot*
Percy sang "When a Man Loves a Woman" –
"Aretha stood *here.*" She requests a bit of tea.
"Get the queen *a drop a' tae,*" a mixer says.
The tin cup judders in her fingers, uncrackable
(pity, if ever a time for the sport of crockery
smashing, this was it). Even her ace producer
can't fathom how for her, each song's a wedding
in a land of no divorce, 'til death does her part.
Being a bride spooks a singer, that and the lustrous
roach due south of her white white sandals.

The Studio: Memphis (2)

From behind glass they watch her. *Turn the track louder*
her hand signals say, *more, more.* The mixer's begging now:
"Stop her, she'll injure herself." Her hairdresser's mouth is sprayed
into an "O." Hours pile on hours. Their world of patch
cables, wires, faders, stories and signal routers could overheat, the whole
joint blow in one pellet of flame and where would the rats be then?
Wexler can read faces well enough, theirs all say – *shut her down.*
He swats them away. Let her hurt

as genius must. The others are scared of the small varnished animal
of song. She doesn't scare him. Much. Though it's hard to watch
a woman murder her own young ears, wear her best dress to hatchet
what's within so song can start from scratch. If this is scratch, it's nothing
they've heard on earth. Feed it to her. Give her the roar she begs for.
Good chance she won't, like it's said of women in labour (reaching
decibels they're never in their lives hit), remember. Count on agony's
amnesia, the racket of a dream.

Fan Mail

They don't have to say they love her but they do. *You sound like menthol cigs,*
I love menthols. Your voice is mint julep. "Son of a Preacher Man" was "our song"
and even though my beloved's gone I weep on the spot whenever it plays on radio.
I saw you at Cranberry Fold Inn, thought you'd be taller.
Thought this. Thought that.
The more you sang the taller you grew. I've been training my eyes, what brand
of mascara do you use? I want to be you. You, Dust (may I call you that),
the only one who could ever reach me. They say you're easy I don't
believe them you couldn't
sing like that if you were. Always it comes down to love.

Love. Love.

The Producer's Poem

...she had an obscure avant-garde genius as her goal.
—Tom Dowd

If he had hair
he'd tear it out.
Hour nine, she records
the same syllable again,
again, again. She makes her art
one syllable at a time and it
hurts to watch. He can't hear a hair
of difference between sounds, it's one tick
of the clock against another.

"That's where you're wrong," she says.
She is, as he supposed, from outer space,
why he worked to snag her in the first place.

She's the sound of elsewhere, the struck note
you don't hear every day. The alien trout
that melts your tongue then poisons you.
It would take so little, now, to throw her back
into the stream, walk
away. He wonders when they might graduate
to a whole word, an entire song.

"When it's *right*," she says. "It's still not right."

The truth is, space beings frighten him,
their power. He steps out for air,

sees the spell her hairdresser
is under, on call all these hours. Same
with her ladies in waiting
beyond the control room,
doing crosswords, smoking,
flipping magazine pages, stirring coffee.
All on alert like she's some deity.
Like she's making them say "love"
over and over
until they get it right.

Festival of Light, England, 1971

(Or, The Day the Queens Crashed the Ball)

The time has come.
The white mice deserve light.
They've lived underground too long.
They're small but many. Above ground
it's spring in Westminster, the lawn hazed blue
with bloom. The Christians are throwing an outdoor
party. The white mice aren't invited, they're going anyway.
They get dressed up, some like House of Lords' wives, some
like lords. The wife-mice look fetching with their scrubbed tiny
ears. The boy-mice, bent on bounding into light dressed like someone
they love, dig through last year's dandelion fluff, make blonde wigs
like Dusty Springfield. There are great furry flurries of preparations,
no time for squeaking, snogging, or parlare. This is it. From office paper
they've collected the mice make hundreds of signs, stick them to old
toothpick ends and

up they come. They storm the lit world's enormous proper party, gnaw the holy
balloons, burst them. The news reports a riot. The *real* Dusty Springfield
watches her telly with joy. The Christians said the small animal
uprising (which spoiled their party) could have been one of
several unfortunate things: *a moving white carpet*
that swept the earth along with it, a malevolent
low-flown freak frost, a rampage
of Hallowe'en or plague
of locusts spurred
on by the devil's
music (pop).

California

She loves the wild
west the moment
she touches down.
So much pink most
adored shade. No
more moors, grim
governess tales.

Here she can cross
lines, slide
like Peggy Lee
right into "Fever."

This town drips
citrus and stars.
Hazy on history she
seems to remember
a gold rush. She'll
rewrite history it's that
kind of country, declare
a Dust Rush
from this
day forward.

II

Bougainvillea

That first morning in America, a floral surf
surged over the garden wall, rolled right
in her direction. She ran to it, feet bare,
nightgown a foaming white wake behind her.
The blooms swayed, scented, labia-like and
since this was Hollywood, light tipped
right on cue, rendered them so magenta she fell
instantly in love. A country where flowers river
down from above, now it was hers. She opened
her arms to the grand garland, it punctured her
everywhere. The day had blood in it, now.
Why had no one warned her about knives strapped
to woody stalks, about thorns? Or whispered
the name she'd hear for years as *bogey-villain.*

Hotels

Let's sing them an anthem, hum them a hymn.
Glory be each numbered door, every last white
towel, even the frayed. Every day is laundry day,
you always come up clean. Hotel bibles know
their place (drawers), they pass no judgment, nor
does the pool, an aqua bowl brimming with faith.
Somewhere, someone stuffs a shower
cap into a small box. A sacred act. Let's hear it
for those paper hats the tumblers wear, for country
stations blurring by as you twirl clock-radio dials
until your own voice washes across the shag carpet.
You're free of history, here. Or, if you *must* have one
it's jolly – a trembling chambermaid seeking your
autograph, her breath small gallops inside her uniform.
Your sheets are smoothed to perfection in the wake
of such moments, garden roses appear on your pillow.
Even the desert rustles up roses. What worlds a simple
word-quartet can hold: *let there be vacancy.*

Fortune

The lucky ones, they're born with tragic
spoons in their mouths. They don't lift
a finger and presto, they're legends. Granted
they got lots of help – Frances Gumm
given enough diet pills to send her straight
to Oz. Edith Piaf raised in a brothel, what
could be better? Norma Egstrom in flight
from her evil stepmother, born again
in Fargo (rising aglow from the chrysalis
as Peggy Lee). What about Mary O'Brien?
Plain old middle-class Mary must work hard
given her mother (unhappy in all the usual
post-war-wife ways). Her father fetching her
at Ealing Tube Stop, still wearing his tax
officer cap. Hardly the stuff of tragedy.
Perhaps it goes beyond spoons or fate or
chance, beyond what you put in your mouth.
Look at her now, she's Dust. Things couldn't
be better, the world having dumped a big
stinking garden square in her lap.

The Plenitude of America

Pills for conking zap-asleep, tabs for waking up,
capsules hailing from the sky, Quaaludes in a cup.
Lozenges for lounges, jellybeans to make you mean,
make you holler at her. Meds meant for a soft forgiving blur.
Dope to drag the song so low, junk to lift it high –
nothing can't be mended here, you only have to try
and pay the Candy Man, he'll soon stroll by.
There's food for every mood, grist
for every whim. "But Dust," they gasped
beside the pool, "*remember?* – you can't swim."

Powder for the wettest whim, just watch –
it makes you buoyant, too. Then there are the Chemists'
aisles – booze zoo – gin and tonic when you're through.
You can't walk to Aspen on Aspirin alone, if only
they'd keep up, grasp her stately mind – consider *time* –
there's *Before* Christ, *After* Christ, why not *During* Christ?
Surely that's *now,* these spinning, sunlit hours, how wide
her eyes: rabbits bounding through the hedge, fan mail
hauled in on a sledge, every moment more surprise.

Three Riddles for Her Neighbourhood

It's a good
neighbourhood,
you can tell
by the gates.
Another week
end, shots
why shots
in this good
neighbourhood,
can anyone
solve this riddle?
"Because it's
America?" *Yes,*
well done, right
on the money
(she must concoct
some wee prize
for this clever
respondent).
Like most riddles
it opens into another
(for insiders this
time) – *where do*
the shots come
from? We give up.
Phil Spector's
garden, his own
private walla sound.
The riddler sips,
airlifts her heart (its
bulletproof vest
tied on tight invested

in this land
of the free). *Ok*
this last riddle
is democratic, for
everyone: what drips
with oxygen, pains
the eardrums
and doesn't stop?

We give up.

Haven't you
been listening? –

The roar of a garden
in America, a good
neighbourhood at week's end.

Good Dust

She's ironed the afternoon
away, her hand
romancing the heat, closer,
scorching her palm.

Before that, she baked
brownies, see them cool
in their stupid square pan
by the pool near the gaggle
of empty martini glasses
she straightens while not
thinking of how little she
sings these days, how so
often now, her voice

simply won't work. Before that
she drank the martinis, someone
had to. She fucking hates
Aerosmith, all they listen
to, now. She scrubbed
the kitchen tiles
until Mary O'Brien's horrid
face shone through, making it
needful to spill something,
anything, all over them.

Before that she beat an angel
food cake, made a wee
game of it, pretended the batter
was the Vatican. The cake

collapsed, had to be tossed
into the pool. It floated
near the chairs and chicken bones.
Then sank, sad angel-stone.

Her sweet Faye will be cross
when she comes home
from the office wanting a dip.
Faye will say, "Well, have you
been a good Dust today?"

Good Dust will smuggle
her red ironing hand into her
apron pocket, will smile,
point to the rainbow wall
of fresh folded blouses.

Laurel Canyon, 1975

Her wrists are no longer safe. The Fiesta plates quake on their shelves.
She's sick of the riche, the burnt hills. She's not riche anymore. As for the pool,
swimming, she never did learn. Fondue forks float amid a molder
of hibiscus petals. Fuck fondue. All the scared little saucers.
She's sung no songs for three years. What's she got?
Gorilla biscuits, sweet interludes, Quaaludes, the girlies in their
tennis whites. Martinis, it's always five o'clock somewhere.
Wind your watch backwards if need be. She's pretty sure
she was, in a previous life, authentic. Like America.
Float down a river, find something real.

The Future (as seen from San Fernando Valley)

Why can't she be like all the other good
drivers, bore her eyes straight
into tomorrow? She'll miss the edges
that way. She's long harboured sympathy
for edges (America's not
about edges). Her foot leadens
on the gas, she'll miss visiting
hours at Chino Prison if she doesn't
hurry. The outlaw-haired woman
waiting there for her (behind glass)
will rough her up with words,
verbal headlocks, it will hurt like hell.

Yellow eyes flicker at the road's rim.
She brakes. They don't like that here.
Coyote. What do coyotes eat? (Her car's
loaded with cat food.) The coyote
wears a diamond-studded collar, doesn't
know who it is. It yelps terrible songs
she can't ignore. She opens her door.

Why can't she ever be on time?
Prisoner 7814 (Women's Wing)
is livid: how could she pick
some dumb fucking animal
over *her, how?* Her curses
careen through glass, lodge
in the singer's heart and the dog
who's not a dog
locked in Dusty's car
in the prison parking lot
claws her leather seats
to shreds.

1979

They found her father when milk
bottles overflowed the front porch.
When it was too late. If Hollywood
wasn't so distant, she'd have flown
to him, smashed each
bottle in his name, for hadn't he
taught her how sound
worked, glass

striking a surface? Hadn't he
said *listen good, girl, you'll only*
hear it once, the shatter's tonal
range. Hadn't he tapped rhythms
on the back of her hand, a kind
of musicological Braille, smacked
her fingers if she got the song wrong?
He had. Soon she never got it wrong.

Medicine

Doctors tell her rest. The Virgin Islands
are a bore, good for nothing but sleep.
She sleeps the sleep of the normal,
toddles to the drive-in. It's nice for a while.
But there's no cure, no transfusion
for confusion. For the sounds that box
her ears:

orchestra strings silken in the extreme boppop gone-for-broke gospel
grit and grind Spector's wall of sound ballads to blast open
hearts of grid-iron even the old Latin babble and twang

How can she hear herself drink with all this noise?
Who is she? How many faces has she?
The only place she finds some peace
is Heathrow, watching planes lower and rise,
rise and lower. The best view's the bar, so much
glass. She wears her dark glasses – if anyone
asks, she's resting. Thinking they should name a drink
after her: Dusty Nail. Dustini. Or for those horrid days
when the sounds simply won't stop, a Bloody Mary O'Brien.

Visit to a Friend's Ranch

She lights lots of candles, submerges in the bath.
Only her face juts above the bubbles. She hopes
bathing will help her voice. She closes
her eyes, counts to ten. When she raises
her lids, she's looking into a goat's yellow gaze.
Its horns meld into a single ponytail of bone.
How did she miss hooves on hardwood?
Once there was no animal

she couldn't hear. "I think you should sing again,"
the goat says. A far candle gutters. She'd wanted
advice, she only wishes it could take some other
form – goats have this way of looking constantly
not amused. The animal pronounces her *lost*, asks
if she intends to wallow in warm suds, hide out
at ranches or die, behind sunglasses, of self-pity.

She arranges her frothy arms along the porcelain
ledge, casual-like, so the goat won't think its words
got to her. She breezes it's all under control. But
the goat goads: then why are her arms all cut?
She sinks them quick. If there's anything she can't
stand, it's a sanctimonious goat, a clever-britches
Billy. Her friend's voice scales the stairs – *Dust,*

need anything? Who were you talking to just now?
Dust calls into the depths: she's not missing a thing,
thanks. Oh, towel. She blinks, she's alone with candles
once more. The room holds no trace of advice. The air
does not resonate with receding clicks of hooves
on hardwood. *Lost?* She needs no goat come back
from the dead to tell her this. Her friend brings towels,

perches on the ledge of the tub. *What sort of reverie has our Dust been in up here?* Bubbles sharpen her ability to lie. "Just remembering ghost stories, animal fables, that sort of thing. Jumbled with Shakespeare from convent school, *Hamlet,* only play I could stomach. The empire was seized by Aerosmith, the ghost was a goat. The prince had perfect antic pitch. Ophelia went flat, then sank."

Nightmare of the Decade

Dodging oranges   running   citrus grenades
at her back the two people she
hates most, orange-fisted, hard on her red platform
heels   a Sunkist orb

hits her spine   hurts   she turns
sure enough it's Mary O'Brien, crucifix a drunk
skipping rope flinging about her fat face
and that bitch Anita Bryant, her aim

Republican-straight. Instead of swishes
their long skirts make pistol-shots when they run
the skirts don't slow them   her own mini's a noose
around her thighs   what gives

last night's nightcaps a few mere screwdrivers   now this
orange hail   pursuers in puffy pioneer blouses
gaining on her

"Mary Go Home" she hollers all jagged
hoping this will help   close behind Anita snarls "*You're* the homo!"
Ahead   an industrial juicer larger than Ealing and
more ugly   she's headed right for the blades   her heart
pummels to pulp
                                        thank Christ and all the virgins she
wakes up bellowing –
                                        "A plague on both your blouses!"

Release

(Santa Monica)

The nice lady finished crying. She was free, the nurses said. She could go home. She shed her patient gown for slacks, silken blouse, long sleeves billowing like violet flags. I don't wish her free or home. Why not? Because she sang in her room. Not loud, but still. A soft spirit voice. The first time I passed her open door, her tones braked my chair. I could only listen, my mouth all gobbed open. Her sound beat church hollow. After her song she said "*Thank you, thank you, you're all much too kind.*" *Who* was too kind? No one else was in the room. The nice lady looked up and saw me, then. Dark glasses covered her eyes. I was one scared hamster. What if she called the nurses? She held out her hand – "Come in, child." I said, "You sing glorious." She smiled, some heaven in it, the best thing that happened to me. Such dainty teeth. I asked could I listen tomorrow. She nodded. Her name? Mary O'Brien but don't call her that. Her talking voice wasn't like anyone I knew. I came every day. She sang lots of songs. I knew some from the radio. She sounded just like the radio. Now she's packing and I won't hear her anymore. She's rising. Tugging off her sunglasses. She has an idea. She winks. I say what. "We're going to a party." I'd no day pass. That didn't stop the free nice lady. I never met anyone so swift. She grabbed her suitcase, shoved my chair out of there, propelled it through all those corridors into a razzle of California sun. She hailed a taxi as if she was magic or had magnets stuck on the ends of her fingers. She told the driver drive us to a *real* car, a limo. I never was in one before. The limo swung us to this big sparkling house where ladies sang through their beautiful hair. Ladies (on day passes?) a tad saucy but some heaven in them, too. I said who are *they*, she told me Labelle. I kept pinching my arm, maybe I'd gone under anaesthetic all this time. Mary O'Brien said, "*Stop* it, don't do that to yourself." We strolled among palms pools fountains of punch and mere minutes earlier we were in a hospital, doctors paged and paged over the intercom now this music these laughing ladies. A man in giant glasses talked to us. He wore a pink suit, rose in his lapel. The nice lady now laughing called him Elton. He called her Dusty. Soon I understood. I sure knew him, I knew *Buh-Buh-Buh*

Benny and the Jets by heart. I just *loved* that and here he stood before me, my mouth catching bubbles and flies. I turned to the free lady then. I said, "Jesus yellow brick road and all the saints *thanks*, Mary." She said "Don't bloody call me that" but she smiled and heaven flopped down over me again.

A Brief History of Disco

Disco – a romance – two incompatibles hook up –
chicken-scratch guitar does the hustle
with some strings. They move into a big
shiny synthesizer, everyone says
it won't last. It won't
still: they wouldn't trade those spinning bits
of mirror
for a whole archive of ballads. Their quavered love
child, Disco, lives the best kind of life,
dizzy, brief, intense,
closet adrip with fresh dry-cleaned white three-piece suits.

Disco (2)

Love to love you Baby. She twirls Donna Summer's vinyl
techno-trek to a fifteen-minute orgasm (one can only
imagine). The disco-haters heap scorn:
"Look, if it takes a whole team of engineers
just to *fake* it,
something's wrong."

They've missed the point. The point
being the sex
inside the engine
sounds real.

The new electronic drums
tickle her. A machine beating a drum, a monkey typing
Shakespeare, why not?
Why *not* step inside the latest sonic appliance?
She's long longed to be peerless as an electric piano and
all you disco-haters: about Donna
doing her thing – you *listened*, didn't you,
you *did* listen
right to the end.

She listened, too.

Various Shows, Late Seventies

(London)

...my whole life is dominated by thoughts of what
it is going to be like, what am I going to wear and will
anybody come to see me.

—Dusty Springfield

The curtains flutter open. She swallows, pushes her roller skates into the light. She hasn't sung for five years, will her voice fail her? She tumbles. Is anyone there to see? Hundreds roar their love. Did she spoil her hair? They don't care. She rises. Smooths her silver slacks. Gives the skates another go. Each tumble the crowd adores her more. Daisies shower her, objects that glitter. They chant *Does Tea, Does Tea.* She doesn't protest too much, dabs her eyes' dark corners. Stagehands unlace her skates, slide her feet into heels that preserve her roller-height. Ten feet tall and hasn't sung a word. Home.

From Buckingham Palace

Apologize. Tell the queen you're sorry. That you royally regret your words spoken in London before opening your mouth to sing. It was wrong to speak lightly of queens in the presence of <u>real</u> royalty. We refer to Princess Margaret, of course, who occupied the royal box that night. Margaret has always been sensitive. Margaret has always been serious. But she is still a woman of ancient blood, and sister of the queen.

You may hold high standing as Queen of Mods or White Soul First Lady or whatever nomenclature they now apply in your direction; nevertheless, your silver throat is hardly above offence. Your flings with the Stars and Stripes, Miss Springfield, have done little for your manners. The Americans have never been known for their eloquence; still, this lamentable state does not grant you free reign to gutter your tongue when on English soil. You are, after all, a British subject. One who sprang from below, the working classes, and strived to better herself. We expected more, even from a singer. We are shocked, saddened. We are not amused. What model do your grievous carryings-on offer today's youth, many of whom, admittedly, are libertine and deluded?

Tell the queen it was never your intention to compare her sister with certain others in attendance at your London concert. We've written it all out for you. You only have to sign. In case any doubts linger as to authenticity, note the wax, the royal seal. No stamp is needed, we've affixed that. The letter requires your most sincere and contrite apology alone.

Sign beside the X on the line below.

X ______________________________ Miss Dusty Springfield

What Has She Done to Deserve This?

If the seventies don't soon end
she'll do it for real. How many more pink tracksuits
must give their lives? (Bloodstains don't leave.)
She'll wallow if she wishes.
They got used, all the sixties singing girls tied
in pretty boxes then spit into supper clubs. Their hair
hasn't been right since. Last she heard, Sandi Shaw
was waiting on tables. One record label gobbled
another and another and no one knew where her
songs were but her, lodged in the holding
tank of her throat
was where they were. She's been raking that throat
with cold toast, slaking it with vodka from a silver
flask. She tells this to the trucker interstated
on a diner-stool beside her, whispers she's really
a famous singer, no, *really*,
she is. His giant steak knife hovers over his red rare
meat, the yellow headlights of his eggs –
"Yeah, *sure*, lady."

The Lost Years

(musings in an unspecified bar)

If she died, no one would notice. Frank Zappa buys milk
down the street, doesn't give her
a second look. "*You*," she'd like to holler his way –
"did *you* duet with Hendrix, well, *did* you?"
Course not. *She* was the one to volley sound back
at Jimmy – "*Mock-ya-king-ya bird-ya-ya-ya*" – his guitar
a screech of light.

If she'd been better
at tragedy perhaps
someone might remember her. John R. Cash
had it right: make the lost years
really damned good and lost. Pick flowers
on gated land, land in jail. Burn down
half a national forest, tell them your truck
did it. Crimes against nature. Her bad
behavior has always been against
herself
        the misdemeanors of a small
has-been, far from home.
They called "Preacher Man" a hit,
ya, well, it had *mistakes*, it had
fucking flaws.

Another voice – a waiter's, glory be –
she must have waved her empty
glass, some service at last. Instead

she gets "Ma'am? Haven't you
had enough? You just asked me if
I sang with Hendrix. Ma'am,
I was barely *born.* I really think
you've had enough."

III

Some Things She Did for Money

Sang inside a cube, crooned through dry ice
wondered what the hell
dry ice *was.* Chirped a ditty to sell
Mother's Pride Bread (if Blossom Dearie
could peddle root beer, *she* could hustle loaves).
Pretended to *like*
Mother's Pride Bread. Sipped a fizzy drink
for Britvic, told the world, in so many words
drink me, sound like me.
Joined the circus by accident (nightclub
gone tacky, that can happen when you're gone
for a long time). The circus had many more
rings than three, depression pills needed
for them all. No one warned her she'd sing
after the midget in the blonde wig silver gown
and before Freddy the Trained Dog
peed in a highly artistic arc. Worst of all
the circus master, dreaming himself
Hugh Hefner, slapping the bottoms
of geyser-bosomed almost-models
so young they couldn't quite place *her*
though she seemed
a *tad familiar* (this can happen
when you're gone).

Checklist for the Early Eighties

Too old too dumpy too pale too many laugh lines frown lines
too advanced too matronly to be exotic too Yankee for the Brits
too Limey for the Americans too young for retro-fitting too
recycled dragged out fagged out too many cigarettes sleepless
nights too much hair spray red tape too many speeding tickets
last calls past last call too many spoiled track suits charts topped
by the voices of others too forgotten teutonically lonely

Not enough time alone not enough paparazzi not enough hits
not enough flattering necklines not enough gin law or order
not enough contract language not enough advances in wigs not
enough slumber not enough to smoke not enough cabaret
imitators not enough rebirth cultural curiosity not enough
compelling reasons not to cry not enough incentives to laugh
not enough tanning salons not enough cake at the health club
cafeteria not enough R-E-S-P-E-C-T for the stateswomen of song.

Toronto, Canada

(from an imaginary journal, 1980-81)

Leather and snow and snow.
Sandblasted brick. World's most
interminable street. Walk, land
in a lake. Some kid swam across,
she heard, to New York. She
understand this. The wind bullies her,
she's a matador's rag in a country
sans mercy. Nash the Slash never
goes out without surgical bandages,
she begins to see why, why no one
knows his true identity (theory goes
he's just a boy from some suburb
trying to stay warm). The streets
are a stew of sound she can't permeate:
glockenspiel, "Lady Marmalade,"
bagpipes. *Toronto.* More like Torsion
of the heart. Tory (never have liquor
shops been so hidden). The street junk
is mean. No wonder she can't sing.
Her teddy bear cowers in a Victorian
garret. The hairdressers don't get her
and some people can't take a bath
without being raided. Then there's that
cold needle probing the sky. Even the folk
songs are ironic, where's the soul? One
direction remains, south. She picks up
her pace, lake looms.

Her Friend Ice

The bowl, commodious, brims with cubes.
She closes her eyes, lowers her face
into it,
its jagged chill
will make much of last night
go away. Understand: this
is no dunk, this
is remedy.
Ritual.

There are tricks for women
with no sleep, submersion in ice
the oldest device in the book.
There is no book

Only this bowl, colour of smooth cream,
a bowl meant for rising dough. Loaded instead
with tiny glaciers.

She won't lift her face
until her cheekbones tingle, until the geography
of yesterday
melts into history. Even if it
means waiting until she can no longer
feel her face. Only then is she
ready for foundation,
only then,
another day.

How To Be Born Again (in the Secular Sense)

A Five-Step Program (by Anonymous)

First you must
admit you're dead. Have the fan letters the flowers
stopped? Do your shoulder pads outsize
your bank account?
Been holding hands with strangers
in church basements? Right, then,
you're ready. Let's begin. You must
become a bird. Concentrate. A phoenix
in blonde plumage, tall boots. Strut a bit,
try out your new legs. Dust yourself off.
You've a pulse? Good news –
you're back. Work that techno-strut,
work it, but keep the whole thing offhand,
it's a motorized ice machine, this new world.
No room for sobbers or wankers. Let's review:
Admit, bird, strut, dust, keep it cool.
Those small lights swirling above your head?
Soon they'll seem natural as stars.

The Publisher's Apology; Or, Who Is Gladys Thong?

We, publisher of *How to Be Born Again*
(a Five-Step Program) apologize for any
confusion or delusion our misprint may
have spawned. The *real* author of *Born*
(secular version) is not Anonymous
at all, but Gladys Thong. Who's this
Miss Thong? No, not naughty underwear,
that's not invented yet. Gladys lives behind
other voices. You've heard her in the backing
tracks for Doris Troy, that Kiki Girl and hosts
of others, you just didn't know it was her.
Miss Thong prefers low profiles. She's even
more modest than Anonymous, no signings
or tours for *her*. If you wish to see her,
look up – not that she's a crow, not our
Gladys. She's of fuller feather, an origin
of species. We'll refund your money
but may we suggest you keep *Born*, first
book ever penned by a member
of the bird kingdom. It could be worth
something someday.

Debbie

Dusty loves Debbie, a love that trumps
all others, love for one's hairdresser.
No matter how awful her voice,
her hair is good. Debbie never fails.

Debbie lives in Boreham Wood
with Andy the mechanic. Some say
"Boredom Wood." Dusty
knows better. She can go there
whenever she likes, curl up with Pebbles
the dog, football on the telly.
Andy doesn't mind. It's real life
with menthols, Big Macs and fries.

Dusty lobbed a hairbrush, once.
Debbie, forehead red from the hit,
forgave her in cockney trembles
that know it's hard for poor Dust,
not sleeping, and all.

Dusty sends a driver to fetch
Debbie and Andy for the game
at Wembley. They won't stop
thanking her, she's sent them
straight to heaven. Dusty calls it
nothing, the least she can do for

Debbie, a warrior with a blow-dryer,
a saint. Debbie says, "Ah, *piss* off,
will ya" before reaching to repair the loose
strand on Dusty's fringe.

Hedgehog

Who can solve the riddle of the eyes?
She can spy a hurt hedgehog
from her moving roadster's wheel
yet faces past row one

are merely blurs (though rapt).
She keeps gloves in her glove box
being more logical
than people think. She pulls over.

The animal is small, all spine
and no action. It can only roll itself
into a ball, hope for the best.
She knows what *that's* like. She sings

"The Look of Love." It fails to snarl.
Soon enough it chomps her leftover
salad in the back seat. She can't read
the signs but somewhere

the road ahead must hold a place
for hurt creatures with musical bents.

Bless This Whoever Whatever

Where lives the healer of fault lines? In some cave
hung with herbs with yellowed news clippings
or right there among them in the dairy aisle?
There must be a healer. Yesterday's lines found
only fault, called her washed up, a has-been
gobbling another tub of orange sherbet.

Now she's a Sixties Icon, happened kind
of sudden. What potion makes *now*
romance *then*, the very thing it spat
away yesterday? When does junk
flip to its opposite? Who calls the hoary
salmon chiefs to lead the spawning young (the old
know the river's bad bits)? What incites
sleek jets to beg the antique flying machines –
Point the way, O wise winged vessels, we're
still frightened of heights.

There must be a wizard. Healer. Lady of Icons.
Whoever you are, you who hold the shaking earth
until it melds back into a single
green seam, *bless* you.

She's a Sixties Icon.
She's still pinching her blubbery arms.
She hasn't got a thing to wear.

That Forgotten Light

Diva-saurus one day, legend the next.
Who can gainsay how it goes around?
She's been driving this or that
coast for years, forgotten by even
the queens. The light
along the freeway is fraught in this
time of tongues lodged in cheeks,
this queer thirst for old chords
crashing into young. The pulse
of tomorrow throbs through her
car radio – futuristic crank-shaft
not without whimsy. Yesterday
her early hit wafted through a mall
elevator, her voice plucked out.
The afternoon-shift bartender,
the philosophical one, said consider
it a flattering form of kidnapping.
Shag *that*, a form of *death*
was what it was, melody's carcass
picked clean. Some boys from
a pet shop want to talk to her,
their song has a hole she alone
can fill. Let them convince her,
just *let* them.

This Ducky Life

She's no stranger to thorns. An adoring rose
lobbed onstage nearly took out her eye.
Another, white, if memory
serves, struck her cheek
buffered by foundation.
Strange how a girl
spends her life
ducking or
making others duck.

Knives rarely remain in one place for long.
Forks have restless tines, keep changing
their tunes. Even empty bottles
of Mateus wine, hip in their hats
of bobbing flame, want to see
how fire looks in flight.

If you love someone, let them know –
throw something. Is that what this
ducky life's about, frequent
flyer points, crockery that
can't keep its place, roses
turned, for an instant,
into birds?

You bet it is.

Ornithology for a Sentimental Planet

Forget all that phoenix
rising nonsense. Sheer
bollocks, the ravings
of sentimental poets
who must make
every crumb myth.
It's a seagull she's been
all along yes queen of gulls
who grew, in the end, wise.
What did she learn from her
trans-ocean flights?
That crumbs aren't worth
getting wet for, it's got to be
the whole loaf. No mere
skimmer tern or fly-by-night, she.
Ornithologists with good ears
mistook her for Sooty Gull
then White-Soul Gull
(yes gulls have souls
after a fashion). Now they've
pegged her, a far rarer
species: the Springfield Gull
known to switch plumage
as the scene demands, a cry
so sweet it can lure
even apostles of science
to the wrecked shores of this
most outrageous planet.

Pulp Fiction

She's long dreamed of being in a movie,
now she is, her voice, at least. A real
American flick, brains splattered
across every surface. Sex and death
and death. She's famous. Press
press her like before, lurk and spring
with their loaded shutters
from the shadows: *Just tell us who*
your lover is, stars don't soak in sunken
baths alone, just give us a name.

She knows them, they've been calling
her fat and bent and lost for years,
their meat-grinder words pressed
into scandal-shaped patties.
She's often wished them
gruesome ends.

Today she'll *give* them a name –
"*Vincent Vega, so there!*
Yes, I slept with Vincent Vega."

The ink-slinging snoops frown, their pupils
spin in their heads –
What kind of idiots did Miss Springfield think them? –
Vincent Vega comes from *Pulp Fiction.*
Vincent Vega isn't even *real.*

Plenty idiots. That's the kind she thinks them.
Wankers with the shortest pens imaginable.
Tiny historians of cruelty.

Motherland

Her collarbone has fallen loose. It jabs at her heart
like a Celtic spear. They say she's well. She'd be well,
the breeze at her back, if not for the spear, the ache
in her breast. She keeps it to herself. Considers ashes.
For the first time in years, wants her Irish mother.
There's a final map to pore over. The Burren coast,
perfect and morose. She rests her boots in bracken.
Profuse, rolling moss. Pins an icy orchid to her coat,
inhales wild thyme. This quiets the spear for a time.
She stands at the edge of the cliffs, imagines her
own ashes tossed, lifted, tiny powdered gulls down-
bound, lofted in slow spirals, to the churn below.
She'd be well to end this way, lovely lilt, then
gone. But not today. The bog man rents her a room
in a castle. She signs in: *Mary O'Brien.* He poaches
eggs for her, sings *O Mary, doan-cha weep doan-cha
mourn.* Off-key but she loves him. Her turret faces
America, promised land. All that sea, so many lost
people. She's been there. She drives to Galway
for *Riverdance.* Cries and cries and the spear
it shows no mercy.

Simon

He can't recall a time before
he loved her. There *was* no
time prior to Dusty. He sang
her songs to the mirror in his
Glaswegian bedroom. She
looked back at him,
    her hand raised in that
    pure aching arc.
That hand allowing so much
grace. He studied her moves –
after all, what is worship
if not doing the right
thing with one's hands? She was
his core of beauty, beckoning
from her side of the looking
glass as in stories
where children step through
into some fierce bright country.

She wrote her name on his arm
charmed that arm and when the ink
    wore down to *us*
his future was sealed.

He stood in for her,
not mere sound checks (she being
above crass functionality) –
    he *was* her, his arms
making those slow waves
    (push away the grief)
his fingers rippling home
to his heart. His vocals, like

hers, about to break
but never quite. She taught him

everything and
            in those final days
after he brought her star
magazines and chips then staggered
back to his car, he prayed for
some new story, one that didn't simply
stand there and watch
            while the hoarse world
            whispered itself down
            to silence.

Harpsden Bottom

So this was it, the final house. Even in her
condition, wisps of tender hair warmed
beneath her wig, the perfection of place
doesn't escape her. Nothing does, even
now. The tiny golfer seen through her
generous bay windows far beyond her
garden's lilt and roll has bogeyed
for three days in a row. Her heart, lit
with sympathy, flies his way. It's more
than a game, no one knows that
like she does. The lawn blues,
some flower, she must
check what kind. Her half-moon chair
sways from a rafter. It has followed her
across the globe and back, adored
pendulum. She reaches for stacked
cucumber sandwiches, morphine tabs.
She, a small figure pegged inside a pink
satin jewel box, a fine feeling and
her houses got mythic the moment
she entered them: Aubrey Walk.
Tarzana. Even the Canyon of Sorrows.
This box of gems, her last, she'll call *Tara.*
Have them cook southern tonight.
They'll joke how her appetite abides
(like all appetites).
Later they'll install her by the window,
switch on hundreds of white lights
strung through the trees, a forest
to glow her
to sleep.

1999

There are just some tasks a highness shouldn't have to undertake
like plan her own funeral. Like not live happy ever after. Cinderella
will never organize a memorial. No burial blueprints for Diana, she
vanished into a tunnel. Grace Kelly's chiffon scarf coiled in wreckage,
last we saw of her. Now here *she* is, a dying star. The details
doing her in. Guest lists. Song sequence. Instructions for police,
where to position their gloved hands, how to stand in drizzle (of this
she has no doubt) as the glass carriage passes, bearing *her*.
Plumed horses, pealing bells. Dimensions of the great white wreath.
Why her cat must at all times be fed low-ash tinned food. She once had
a secretary for all this. Now she's her own undertaker, her own lowness.

Last Day

Even icons have last days.
Who should be standing there –
right there on the drizzled lawn among the bumper
crocus crop but Mary O'Brien, drenched,
spectacled in her convent-school jumper
still middle-class to a hopeless degree
still grasping that dumb field-hockey stick.
The stick isn't raised. It's held
in horizontal truce, parallel to the earth.
Mary Isobel Catherine Bernadette O'Brien –
Christ, how many handles can one girl *have*?
March – England's trial by water.
Mild enough for open windows, too wet
to play. The schoolgirl stands
submerged, not sad.
Rain varnishes her hair to her head
and Lord knows the kid could use
a good combing. The sky shifts,
reveals some white thing near Mary,
a flag (pair of knickers) tied halfway
down a pole. Clouds shuffle, the day
may be fair, after all. Miraculous,
these turns of weather. Blessed
be open windows. Mary O'Brien's hand,
her whole arm, undulates through moist
spring, beckons. After everything,
can she still wish to play? Seems she does.
Dust isn't afraid, Mary always *was*
ghastly at sports even a wasted icon

could clean her clock the rain
resumes the girl shimmers out there
drops her stick opens her arms sings
gospel in perfect pitch the kid
has real potential

Notes on the Poems

Dusty Springfield, sometimes known as the White Queen of Soul, was born Mary Isobel Catherine Bernadette O'Brien in 1939 in West Hampstead, London. Raised Catholic, she attended convent schools. During her teenage years, often feeling overshadowed by her brother, she grew determined to make it as a singer; this meant re-inventing herself and leaving Mary O'Brien behind. She joined the Lana Sisters in 1958, and in the early sixties, she joined The Springfields and took the name Dusty Springfield. She then embarked on a solo career resulting in hit songs like "Son of a Preacher Man," "I Only Want to Be with You," "Wishin' and Hopin'," "Stay Awhile," and numerous others. Dusty had a longstanding love affair with America, with soul music, Motown, and Hollywood. Her 1969 album, *Dusty in Memphis*, is considered a classic of twentieth-century popular music.

Dusty was widely known as an obsessive musical perfectionist. In the early seventies, she moved to Los Angeles. She spent fifteen turbulent years there during a time of radical changes in the recording industry, not least of which were the disco invasion and the rise of hard rock. She spent a brief period in Toronto in the early eighties. Feeling left behind and largely forgotten, Dusty struggled with various addictions during the seventies and eighties. To worsen matters, the British press had often been unkind to her, and homophobic attitudes prevailed. Dusty's fortunes began to change in the late eighties when The Pet Shop Boys sought her out to sing a solo track on their song "What Have I Done to Deserve This?" Her music was also repopularized after the release of the movie *Pulp Fiction.* She spent the last years of her life in England. Dusty Springfield died from cancer on March 2, 1999, a few weeks short of her sixtieth birthday. She received the OBE (Order of the British Empire) and was also inducted into America's Rock and Roll Hall of Fame.

Throughout the poems, Mary O'Brien refers to Dusty Springfield's real name and, in many ways, her tortured alter-ego.

Gladys Thong was a pseudonym Dusty Springfield sometimes used when singing backing vocals for her friends.

The epigraph to the poem "The Gospel Truth" is taken from Warren Zanes's *Dusty in Memphis.* New York: Continuum Books, 2003, pages 84-5.

The epigraph to the poem "The Springfields" is taken from Lucy O'Brien's *Dusty: The Classic Biography* (Updated and Revised). London: Sidgwick & Jackson, 2000, page 38.

The epigraph to "The Producer's Poem" is taken from Lucy O'Brien's *Dusty: The Classic Biography* (Updated and Revised). London: Sidgwick & Jackson, 2000, page 124.

"Festival of Light" refers to a Christian movement that promoted traditional family values. In 1971, this group held a meeting in Westminster Abbey. Their meeting was stormed by members of the Gay Liberation Front who dressed up as nuns and released mice in the streets of London.

The epigraph to "Various Shows, Late Seventies" is taken from Edward Leeson's *Dusty Springfield: A Life in Music.* London: Robson Books, 2001, page 139.

"Simon" was inspired by Simon Bell, backing singer and long-time friend of Dusty Springfield.

"Debbie" was inspired by one of Dusty Springfield's hairdressers, Debbie Dannell.

Several of the poems make reference to animals. Dusty Springfield was an ardent lover of cats and other animals. She was involved, for a time, in the rescue of abandoned animals.

Acknowledgements

I am grateful to the Banff Centre for providing writing space. Thanks to St. Francis Xavier University for support to attend a self-directed writing residency at the Banff Centre in April–May, 2007. I was also fortunate to receive encouragement, while writing, revising, and reading from this collection, from Nancy Mattson, Jen Alexander, Jeff Park, Billeh Nickerson, Carolyn Smart, David Lynes, Colleen Murphy, Sheri-D Wilson, Corinna Wagner, Jennifer Londry, Donna Kane, Holly Luhning, Jennifer Still, Leona Theis, the Berg family, and Chris Frazer. Special thanks and multiple toasts to my editor Melanie Little for believing in this collection, and for all her hard work in bringing it to fruition.

"A Brief History of Disco" and "Disco (2)" were published in *Forget Magazine.* "Hotels" was published in *The Literary Review of Canada.* Thanks to editors Kent Bruyneel and Molly Peacock.

This is a work of imagination. However, various sources provided useful background material. These include Warren Zanes's *Dusty in Memphis* (2003); Edward Leeson's *Dusty Springfield: A Life in Music* (2001); Penny Valentine and Vicki Wickham's *Dancing with Demons: The Authorized Biography of Dusty Springfield* (2000); Lucy O'Brien's *Dusty: The Definitive Biography* (updated and revised, 2000); Patricia Julianna Smith's "'You Don't Have to Say You Love Me': The Camp Masquerades of Dusty Springfield" in Smith's edited anthology *The Queer Sixties* (1999); Annie Randall's *Dusty: Queen of the Postmods* (2008); *Dusty Springfield: Reflections* (DVD, 2003); *Dusty Springfield: Live at the Royal Albert Hall* (DVD, 2005); *Full Circle: The Life and Music of Dusty Springfield* (VHS, 1997); various websites.

It's Hard Being Queen: The Dusty Springfield Poems is Jeanette Lynes' fourth collection of poetry. Her previous collections are *Left Fields* (Wolsak and Wynn, 2003, shortlisted for the Pat Lowther Award), *The Aging Cheerleader's Alphabet* (Mansfield Press, 2003), and *A Woman Alone on the Atikokan Highway* (Wolsak and Wynn, 1999). Her awards include the Ralph Gustafson Poetry Prize, the Bliss Carman Award, and first prize in the *Grain* Postcard Story Competition. She has been a visiting artist / writer-in-residence at Queen's University, Northern Lights College in Dawson Creek, and the Saskatoon Public Library, as well as a faculty member at St. Francis Xavier University and the Sage Hill Writing Experience. She is currently co-editor of *The Antigonish Review.*

Jeanette Lynes grew up on a farm in Alice Munro country while "Son of a Preacher Man" played on transistor radios everywhere.